**W9-BSE-622**

AN IMAGINATION LIBRARY SERIES

**WORLD'S LARGEST**

# SNAKES

# Scrub Pythons

by Valerie J. Weber

**Gareth Stevens Publishing**
A WORLD ALMANAC EDUCATION GROUP COMPANY

Please visit our web site at: www.garethstevens.com
For a free color catalog describing Gareth Stevens Publishing's
list of high-quality books and multimedia programs,
call 1-800-542-2595 (USA) or 1-800-387-3178 (Canada).
Gareth Stevens Publishing's fax: (414) 332-3567.

Library of Congress Cataloging-in-Publication Data available upon request
from publisher. Fax (414) 336-0157 for the attention of the Publishing
Records Department.

ISBN 0-8368-3657-X

First published in 2003 by
**Gareth Stevens Publishing**
A World Almanac Education Group Company
330 West Olive Street, Suite 100
Milwaukee, WI 53212 USA

Text: Valerie J. Weber
Cover design and page layout: Scott M. Krall
Series editor: Jim Mezzanotte
Picture Researcher: Diane Laska-Swanke

Photo credits: Cover, pp. 7, 15 © Hans & Judy Beste/Ardea London Ltd.; p. 5
© P. Morris/Ardea London Ltd.; pp. 9, 13 © Michael & Patricia Fogden; pp. 11, 19
© Chris Mattison; p. 17 © David & Diane Armbrust; p. 21 © Craig Pelke

Printed in the United States of America

1 2 3 4 5 6 7 8 9 07 06 05 04 03

*Front cover:* **The skin of a scrub python has beautiful patterns that look like tiles laid out in a design.**

# TABLE OF CONTENTS

Words that appear in the glossary are printed in **boldface**
type the first time they occur in the text.

# A Jewel of a Snake

The scrub python gets its name from one of the places where it lives. In northern Australia and New Guinea, this giant snake slithers through **tropical** forests and grasslands, but it also lives in scrublands — grassy areas covered with short trees and bushes.

This snake is also called the amethystine python because of the purple markings that cover its yellow-brown skin. Amethyst is a purple crystal often used to make jewelry.

In the sunlight, a scrub python shines with the colors of the rainbow. As the Sun strikes ridges in each of its **scales**, the ridges break the light into separate colors, much like a **prism** does. You can see the scrub python's scales sparkle.

In this photo, you can see the purple splotches that give the scrub python its other name, the amethystine python. See how its scales sparkle, like jewelry!

# The Slim Giant

The scrub python is slender compared to other giant snakes, but it is still long. It usually grows to a length of 10 to 12 feet (3 to 3.7 meters). Some scrub pythons, however, have grown much longer. The largest scrub python ever reported measured 28 feet (8.5 m) long!

Unlike many other snakes, a scrub python has a large head that is much wider than the rest of its body. Its lips have deep **pits** that can sense the body heat of nearby animals. Bars of color crisscross some scrub pythons' backs, and stripes and blotches mark their necks.

The pits on a scrub python's lips let the snake know if dinner or danger is close to it, by sensing the body heat of nearby animals.

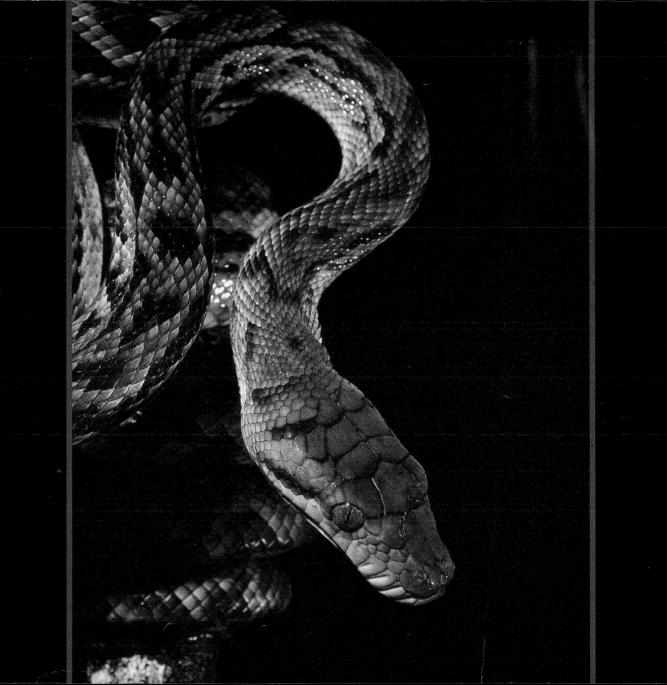

# Smooth Traveler

A scrub python slips smoothly across rocky ground and into the forest. Imagine the control it has over muscles in different parts of its body as it travels across two very different surfaces. Its front might be climbing up a tree while its rear is still moving across gravel!

The scrub python moves like a caterpillar, though unlike the caterpillar, its body does not leave the surface it is on. Muscles on each side of the scrub python move a part of its belly scales forward. The scales dig into the ground underneath the snake's body, and the muscles help push off. While one set of belly scales is pushing forward, another set is ready to dig in and push.

Markings on the scrub python's skin help it blend into the colors of the forest floor. The snake can move in a straight line or with a curving movement.

# Look Ma, No Ears!

Scrub pythons, like all other snakes, do not hear the way you do. They do not have anything to hear with on the outside of their head — no ears!

Have you ever heard music so loud, you can feel **vibrations** come up through the ground and into your feet? A snake "feels" sound the same way. Instead of hearing sound through the air, a snake feels the vibrations of sound through the ground.

The vibrations pass through bones in its head to tiny bones in its inner ears. These bones send information to its brain so the snake knows when **prey** or danger is near.

Scrub pythons and other snakes do not hear well, but they do make noises. These noises are warnings to other animals to stay away.

# Hunting Around

Scrub pythons can hunt on land, in trees, or in the water. They are great climbers, and they will rest in trees for a long time to wait for their prey. With its long tail, a scrub python can hang down from a tree and strike quickly at passing prey.

These snakes can also hold their breath a long time underwater and can keep their eyes open as they swim. Clear, watertight skin covers the scrub python's eyes, but it cannot close its eyes or blink. A scrub python can remain in the water for twenty to forty-five minutes.

Scrub pythons that live in forests are usually darker than scrub pythons that live in grasslands. Darker colors help them hide from enemies or prey.

# Prey for a Scrub Python

A scrub python hunts at **dusk** or at night. With its large, golden eyes, the scrub python can see well in the dim light of early evening.

The scrub python has few enemies and plenty of food. Larger scrub pythons can eat kangaroos and **wallabies** when they can catch them, but most of a scrub python's prey are much smaller. Scrub pythons eat fruit bats, possums, and rats, as well as chickens and other tame animals. These snakes also dine on the pademelon, a kind of small kangaroo.

This scrub python is waiting for prey to pass by it. Perhaps a fruit bat will swoop near it and become the snake's next meal!

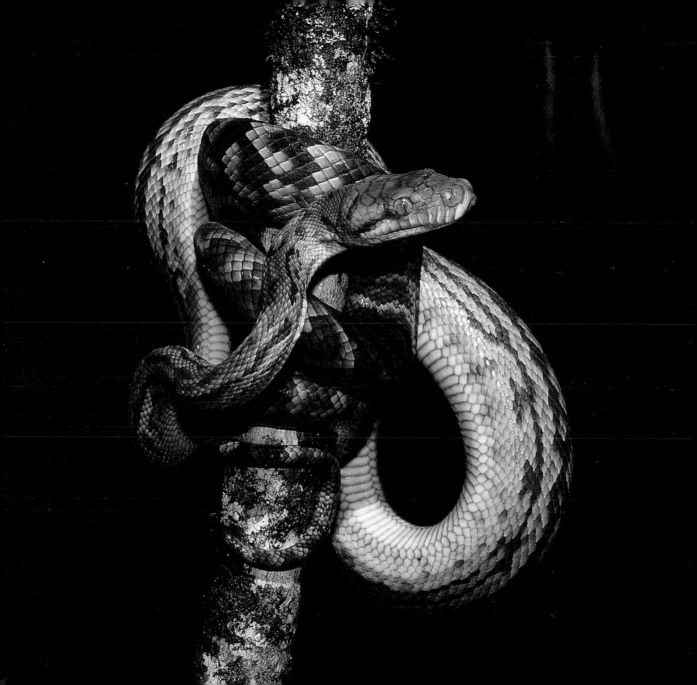

# Open Wide!

After the scrub python grabs its prey with its long teeth, it wraps three or more **coils** around the animal and squeezes tightly. When the prey has **suffocated**, the scrub python opens its mouth wide and begins to "walk" its jaws over the animal.

Like all other snakes, a scrub python's jaws are not connected by bone the way your jaws are. A snake's upper and lower jaw are joined only by a **tendon**, which stretches like a rubber band. The jaws of a snake can stretch apart, so it can open its mouth very wide and swallow an animal much larger than its own head.

Time for dinner! This python has begun swallowing a red-legged pademelon. Believe it or not, the python eventually will swallow the entire animal.

# A Bigger Body For a Bigger Meal

The scrub python's body also gets bigger to take in a large meal.  While your ribs are connected to your backbone in back and your breastbone in front, the ribs of this snake are only connected at the back, so its belly can expand around its food.

The snake's scales and folds of skin overlap, and they can also spread apart to make more room for dinner.  A scrub python's **windpipe** can stick all the way out of its mouth, like a **snorkel**.  Even if the snake has a huge meal in its mouth, its windpipe takes in air so it can breathe.

Some people think snakes are slimy.  But unless a snake has just come out of the water, its skin feels dry and smooth as silk.

# Danger from Humans

Some people hunt and kill scrub pythons for their skin or meat or to use for medicine.  Many people are also afraid of scrub pythons and other snakes and kill the snakes for no reason.  They run the snakes over with their cars while the snakes warm themselves on the road.

Before the 1940s, people hunted so many scrub pythons for their beautiful skins that the snakes almost became **extinct**.  Australia made some of the first laws in the world to protect giant snakes.

This scrub python and its keeper seem to trust each other.  Scrub pythons do well in zoos if they are handled carefully.

# MORE TO READ AND VIEW

**Books (Nonfiction)**      *Fangs!* (series). Eric Ethan (Gareth Stevens)
*Pythons. Animal Kingdom* (series). Julie Murray (Abdo & Daughters)
*Pythons. Animals & the Environment* (series). Mary Ann McDonald
   (Capstone Press)
*Pythons. Naturebooks* (series). Don Patton (Child's World)
*Pythons. Really Wild Life of Snakes* (series). Doug Wechsler
   (Rosen Publishing Group)
*Pythons. Snakes* (series). James E. Gerholdt (Checkerboard Library)
*Pythons and Boas: Squeezing Snakes.* Gloria G. Schlaepfer and
   Mary Lou Samuelson (Franklin Watts, Inc.)
*Snakes.* Seymour Simon (Bt Bound)

**Books (Fiction)**       *How Snake Got His Hiss.* Marguerite W. Davol (Orchard Books)
*I Need a Snake.* Lynne Jonell (Putnam Publishing Group)
*Snake Camp.* George Edward Stanley (Golden Books)

**Videos (Nonfiction)**    *Amazing Animals Video: Scary Animals.* (Dorling Kindersley)
*Fascinating World of Snakes.* (Tapeworm)
*Predators of the Wild: Snake.* (Warner Studios)
*Snakes: The Ultimate Guide.* (Discovery Home Video)

# PLACES TO WRITE AND VISIT

Here are three places to contact for more information:

**Black Hills Reptile Gardens**
P.O. Box 620
Rapid City, SD  57709
USA
1-800-355-0275
**www.reptile-gardens.com**

**Melbourne Zoo**
Parkville, Victoria
Australia 3052
61-3-9285 9355
**zvdl@zoo.org.au**

**Roger Williams Park Zoo**
1000 Elmwood Avenue
Providence, RI  02907
USA
1-401-785-3510
**www.rwpzoo.org**

# WEB SITES

Web sites change frequently, but we believe the following web sites are going to last. You can also use good search engines, such as **Yahooligans!** [**www.yahooligans.com**] or **Google** [**www.google.com**], to find more information about scrub pythons. Here are some keywords to help you: *amethystine python, Australian snakes, New Guinea snakes,* and *reptiles.*

**www.anhs.com.au/diversion_4.htm**
At the *Australian Natural History Safari* site, you can see photographs of an amethystine, or scrub, python swallowing its prey!

**www.rwpzoo.org/what_to_see/australasia/ australasia_scrubpython.htm**
Visit *Scrub Python Snake* from the Roger Williams Park Zoo's web site to learn where the scrub python lives, what it eats, and how it hatches its eggs. See a photograph, too.

**www.totaltravel.com/travelsites/ australianreptiles**
The scrub python is Australia's longest snake. The Australian Reptile Centre Canberra has one, and you can see a photograph of it here.

**www.vpi.com/5VPIBreeders/ ScrubPython/ScrubPython.htm**
Three close-up photographs, plus many interesting facts, make *Scrub Python* a site worth visiting. Learn where scrub pythons are found, how large they grow, and what traits make them unique.

# GLOSSARY

You can find these words on the pages listed. Reading a word in a sentence helps you understand it even better.

**coils** (KOYLZ) — the circles a snake can form with its body  16

**dusk** (DUSK) — the time of day just before the Sun goes down  14

**extinct** (ex-TINKT) — completely gone from Earth, with none of that particular kind of animal alive anymore  20

**pits** (PITZ) — hollow places on the surface of the body  6

**prey** (PRAY) — animals that are hunted by other animals for food  10, 12, 14, 16

**prism** (PRIZ-uhm) — a piece of clear glass or crystal that breaks up a ray of light into the colors of a rainbow  4

**scales** (SKAYLZ) — small, stiff plates, made mostly of the same material as human hair and nails, that cover a snake's skin  4, 8, 18

**snorkel** (SNORE-kuhl) — a tube that a person can breathe through underwater  18

**suffocated** (SUF-uh-kay-tid) — died from having no air to breathe  16

**tendon** (TEN-dun) — a strong, flexible band of tissue that attaches a muscle to a bone  16

**tropical** (TROP-ih-cull) — being in a part of the world where the temperature is always warm and plants usually grow year-round  4

**vibrations** (vy-BRAY-shunz) — very fast back and forth movements  10

**wallabies** (WAH-luh-beez) — kangaroos that are small or medium-sized  14

**windpipe** (WYND-pipe) — a tube in the body that carries air from the mouth and nose to the lungs  18

# INDEX